MAGGIE
STIEFVATER

MAGGIE STIEFVATER

ERIN STALEY

ROSEN
PUBLISHING®

New York

Published in 2014 by The Rosen Publishing Group, Inc.
29 East 21st Street, New York, NY 10010

Copyright © 2014 by The Rosen Publishing Group, Inc.

First Edition

Library of Congress Cataloging-in-Publication Data

Staley, Erin.
Maggie Stiefvater/Erin Staley.—First edition.
    pages cm.—(All About the Author)
Includes bibliographical references and index.
ISBN 978-1-4777-1762-2 (library binding)
1. Stiefvater, Maggie, 1981—Juvenile literature. 2. Women
authors, American—Biography—Juvenile literature.
3. Young adult fiction—Authorship—Juvenile literature.
I. Title.
PS3619.T53548Z87 2014
813'.6—dc23
[B]
                                                    2013014577

Manufactured in the United States of America

CPSIA Compliance Information: Batch #W14YA: For further information, contact Rosen Publishing, New York,
New York, at 1-800-237-9932.

CONTENTS

Considered a "superstar author" of popular young adult and urban fantasy books, *New York Times* best-selling author Maggie Stiefvater has captivated readers with her tales of homicidal fairies, shape-shifting werewolves, missing Welsh kings, and Irish water horses.

As a child, Stiefvater had a long list of things she wanted to be when she grew up. Fighter pilot, best-selling author, radio DJ, comedian, show jumper, and cartoonist were just some of the professions that topped the list. Once Stiefvater was old enough to work, her list of occupations rivaled that of her childhood to-dos. Becoming a calligraphy instructor, wedding musician, technical editor, and equestrian artist paid the bills, but in the end, she couldn't resist the lifelong itch to become a best-selling writer.

Having written over thirty novels by the time she was in college, Stiefvater was sure to grow in her abilities. She was an avid reader and educated herself on the talents and skills of other notable authors. Diana Wynne Jones, her author-hero, inspired Stiefvater's fantasy fiction with serious plots and humorous predicaments. Susan Cooper inspired the setting of mood, M. T. Anderson the use of voice, and Jane Yolen the inclusion of folktales. While she spent hours trying to write like them,

To avoid boring her audience—one of her biggest fears—Maggie Stiefvater uses dry humor, unique props, and zany antics to keep her appearances entertaining and memorable.

Stiefvater finally discovered her own eccentric voice. What she once thought was "too weird" now makes her work all that more appealing to teens and adults. Her fearlessness as an author earned her fans from all over the world.

With creative time management, a supportive husband, and a network of helpful family members close by, Stiefvater chiseled out writing time in her busy schedule. And like her author-heroes, she hoped to offer emotionally gripping stories that only she could spin—stories of nature, animals, myth, and magic. An author with what she calls a "Peter Pan complex," Stiefvater chose to write for teens. Their fresh approach to adventures excited her while their uncertainty and angst compelled her to tackle issues that many teens face. If anything, Stiefvater wants her novels to resonate with readers, inspiring them to want more out of life, even if they can't picture what that is just yet.

Today, Stiefvater's career is on the rise with book deals, movie contracts, tours, and a thriving social media presence. She connects with her readership by sharing writing tidbits, personal stories, videos, art, music, and, of course, announcing upcoming book and tour events.

In the following sections, you will learn the background and writing techniques of Maggie Stiefvater. You will see how her work encompasses her love of art, music, and writing, producing a multimedia experience for her ever-growing readership. Finally, you will discover the wealth of how-to information and the world of possibilities that Stiefvater shares with her loyal fans. She believes that one must be smitten with the act of writing, even to the point of appreciating its instability, to enjoy its benefits. By doing this herself, Stiefvater has conquered the best-seller lists time and time again.

ONE

BETWEEN THE STACKS

Heidi Hummel, who would someday change her name and eventually become best-selling YA author Maggie Stiefvater, was born in Harrisonburg, Virginia, on November 18, 1981. The second child of Dr. Keith Bydler Hummel and Penella Hummel, it was evident from an early age that Maggie was smart, determined, and headstrong. She refused to conform to authority and as a youngster was kicked out of preschool for standing on her cot and refusing to take a nap. A self-proclaimed "Navy brat," Maggie and her family moved countless times because of her father's commitment to the U.S. Navy. Petite and obstinate, young Maggie continued to march to the beat of her own Irish drum. She was often found wearing black turtlenecks and, when

For Maggie Stiefvater, music, art, and writing are intertwined. She uses principles from each to enhance the creativity of all three. Puck from *A Midsummer Night's Dream* is portrayed in this painting.

asked why, she would proudly declare that she was "mourning the death of modern society." She is known for mimicking the mischief of Puck from William Shakespeare's *A Midsummer Night's Dream*. Maggie also took her aggression out on her classmates by throwing punches. With antics like these, it wasn't long before her parents began to homeschool their headstrong sixth-grader and her siblings. Maggie didn't seem to mind the change since she was both resourceful and driven. When educational materials were delivered to their home, her parents quickly passed them to Maggie. She would read the teacher's manual and complete a month's worth of schoolwork in a week. This freed her up to pursue those things that interested her, such as art, music, reading, and, of course, writing.

Because Mrs. Hummel was an artist and musician, creativity was encouraged within the family. Maggie, her sisters, and her brothers learned to play the piano at very young ages. Irish music was a favorite in the Hummel household. As a result, Maggie learned to play the guitar, tin whistle, Irish harp, and a bodhran drum. She eventually competed with the Scottish Highland bagpipes as a high school student. Her siblings also played multiple instruments, causing Maggie to liken her musical family to the von Trapps in *The Sound of Music*.

NATURE LOVER

Maggie was enamored with nature. She would spend hours engrossed in National Geographic programs that featured animals in exotic habitats. Whenever her parents wanted to pull her away from the television, they would announce creature sightings in the woods, and off she would go in search of them. During family vacations in North Carolina, Maggie would often stare out at the rolling waves of the Atlantic Ocean. She had nearly drowned as a child and was fascinated by the ocean's beauty and danger. The combination inspired her to dream up stories of mighty horses bounding from the foamy waves. Often these stories made it onto the pages of Maggie's writing. Even though she wanted to be everything from a fighter pilot to a trial lawyer, she ultimately dreamed of becoming a best-selling author. Maggie longed to lose her readers in the mood of her stories. She was so consumed with the idea that she created a catalog of future books she intended to write. The catalog was then distributed among her relatives so that they could preorder their own copies.

She scoured the library stacks for inspiration, first grabbing any book with a "fantasy" unicorn sticker on the spine. Spellbound, Maggie couldn't

Maggie Stiefvater considers herself to be "horse-crazy" and includes these majestic creatures in her many paintings and literary works. She celebrates the beauty and danger of water horses in *The Scorpio Races*.

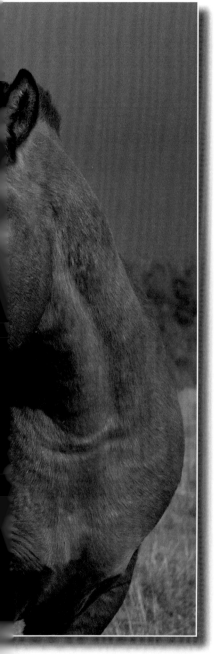

get enough of the old magic that first appeared to be superstitious until it suddenly turned very dark and very real. She was taken with the dramatic tales of Katharine Briggs's *An Encyclopedia of Fairies: Hobgoblins, Brownies, Bogies, and Other Supernatural Creatures.* Obsessed with homicidal fairies, twelve-year-old Maggie always worked them into her writing. She even stood beneath a beech tree with four-leaf clovers in hand to meet them. The fairies never appeared.

Although Maggie considered her parents to be strict, she and her siblings were allowed to have any kind of animal they wanted as long as they could earn the money to buy it. When Maggie was thirteen years old, she and her sister worked all summer to buy two off-the-track racehorses. The girls took care of the retired horses, even during the frosty mornings of a Virginia winter. They would ride bareback, but the horses tended to lean toward the left, making the ride very dangerous. Much like her fascination with the ocean, Maggie was in awe of the beauty of these horses and their ability to harm her. She couldn't get enough of Marguerite Henry's *Misty of Chincoteague*, Walter Farley's *The Black Stallion*, and Bonnie Bryant's *The Saddle Club* series. The girl-and-an-animal element appealed to Maggie's fascination with beauty and danger. She also read veterinarian James Herriot's nonfiction books about the lives of animals and their owners. She loved the timeless nature of old-fashioned adventure stories. Maggie read books about mythology, enjoying the supernatural elements that terrorized the main characters. Of course, she had to read the award-winning books. They were always stamped with one of the three most prestigious YA literary medals—Caldecott, Newbery, and Printz.

LITERARY INFLUENCES

For Maggie, Lloyd Alexander's *The Black Cauldron* series introduced the wonderful world of enchantments. C. S. Lewis's *Narnia* series showed her the possibilities of inventing another world. Madeleine L'Engle's books used mathematics and science to make magic, while Audrey Niffenegger's work brought

Despite her dyslexia as a youngster, Diana Wynne Jones wanted to be a writer. She attended lectures by C. S. Lewis and J. R. R. Tolkien as a university student and went on to become an award-winning author.

her to tears. Diana Wynne Jones, Maggie's author-hero, blended serious subject matter with humor. *Charmed Life*, *The Lives of Christopher Chant*, *Fire and Hemlock*, *Archer's Goon*, and *The Ogre Downstairs* introduced her to mythology. She read *Dogsbody* back to back six times. But it was Susan Cooper's *The Dark Is Rising* series that had the most profound effect on her. This collection is five contemporary fantasy novels for young adults that blend Welsh mythology and fantasy in a realistic world.

Inspired by the volumes of books she read, Maggie wove their literary lessons into her own stories. While her parents encouraged her writing, her father Dr. Hummel, explained that being a writer was not a lucrative profession. Maggie did not let this discourage her. Books changed her perspective of the world, and that's what she wanted to do for her readers. By the time Maggie was sixteen, she was submitting her manuscripts to publishers. However, she was bored with school. Ultimately, she wanted to drop out but was persuaded to stick it out long enough to pursue her General Equivalency Diploma (GED). That same year, Maggie made a major change. She told Rick Margolis of SchoolLibraryJournal.com:

> *I disliked my name for a long time. But the catalyst was when I walked into an eye*

A FINE LINE BETWEEN BRILLIANCE AND DEVIANCE

Maggie Stiefvater considered herself to be a "small and black-hearted child." She remembers her parents' frustration with her lack of focus and nonconformist attitude. However, they decided to homeschool their children, helping her avoid labels such as "rebel" and "anarchist," as well as the common ADD/ADHD diagnosis found in traditional schools. Stiefvater later learned that she was simply trying to find her place in the world. She saw that this rang true with the teens she addressed during her book tours. All too often, adults labeled teens that did not fit societal norms, and those teens believed them.

Stiefvater had always tried to address this issue in her novels, but when she was invited to speak on the topic at the TEDxNASA conference, she couldn't resist. "How Bad Teens Become Famous People" was the title of the twelve-minute presentation, and she shared anecdotes from her childhood. Once labeled as a rebellious and anarchist youth, Stiefvater was now labeled as "freethinking" and "eccentric." The only difference? Perspective. It changes the way we look at people and situations. Stiefvater encouraged teens to forget their labels and urged adults to lose the tendency to label teens because, as she says in her presentation, "There's a really fine line between brilliance and deviance."

doctor's appointment and the receptionist said, 'Heidi Hummel. What a great name! It sounds like a figure skater!' I got in the car and I told my mom, 'Mom, I'm changing my name,' and because I was named after one of my dad's ex-girlfriends, she said yes. I'm really sad to say that I was a very contrary child, so I named myself Margaret, after Margaret Thatcher [the British Prime Minister from 1979–1990], because everyone hated her.

COLLEGE BOUND

Maggie went on to attend Mary Washington College, a liberal arts college located in Fredericksburg, Virginia. She looked forward to the opportunity to spread her wings and pursue her dreams. She had written over thirty novels by the time she had entered college—four Irish Republican Army (IRA) thrillers, one historical blockade runner novel, and one high fantasy novel about impassioned enchanters fighting among civil unrest. It didn't take long for Maggie to consider herself different from her peers. She knew the others thought of her as being an "ice princess" during the first few years of college. But inside, she was just shy and eccentric. Things eventually changed for her as she got involved in extracurricular activities. She played

While at Mary Washington College, Maggie Stiefvater learned the value of research. She used it to add realism to her books. While writing *The Scorpio Races*, Stiefvater visited notable cliffs in the United States and Europe.

with the college pipe band, competed in Highland bagpipe competitions, and worked in a Made in Virginia shop. Maggie played gigs with her Celtic band, Ballynoola. They toured within a three-state radius and even recorded an album called *Driven to Distraction*. When it was time to declare a major, she wanted to pursue music, art, and writing. Yet, when she auditioned for piano classes, she was told she wasn't good enough. When Maggie tried the art department, she was told her portfolio did not meet their level of sophistication. And when she submitted to the creative writing department, she was turned away because they thought her samples did not show promise. However, she was not discouraged. She loved the romanticism of adventure, nature, mythology, and epic fantasy and decided to major in early British history.

In August 2001, nineteen-year-old Maggie met paramedic Edward Stiefvater (pronounced "Steve-Otter"). He came into the Made in Virginia store. She was covering for a coworker who couldn't come in that day, and Edward was there because of a change in shifts at work. He brought a bumper sticker up to the counter where Maggie was reading her book. Before they knew it, the two were talking and laughing. Edward asked her for a date, and in her mischievous way, she dared him to give her a good reason why she should join him. The following day, he brought her a pink rose bud, and again, she playfully responded by saying she preferred yellow. A few days later, a bundle of yellow roses were delivered to the store. Maggie finally agreed to join Edward for ice cream. They spent several hours talking—she about adventures with her Jetta and he telling Betty Boop jokes. The two left holding hands. A month and a half later, Maggie and Edward were engaged. At age twenty-one, Maggie married Edward. In 2003, Maggie graduated from Mary Washington College with a bachelor of arts degree. Although her adviser tried to convince her to pursue a doctor of philosophy (Ph.D.), she had big literary dreams. She was going to become a best-selling YA author.

TWO

COOKIE DOUGH AND SWEET TEA

After college, Maggie Stiefvater began a nine-to-five job for a federal contractor, but she detested working in an office. Although she and Edward were living on a shoestring budget, she was ready to live a life filled with creativity and passion. Stiefvater told Scholastic Canada:

...One day I went in and said, "I'm sorry, this is my two-weeks notice, [sic] I'm quitting to become an artist." And of course, I hadn't been an artist before then and I don't think I was very good then either, but I just decided that was the way to go. And so my boss looked at me and he said, "Well, Maggie, when you want your job back, when you can't make a living, it's always here for you." And

you know what, I made my living in that first year and never looked back, and I will never ever have a job with a cubicle.

MAGGIE STIEFVATER, ARTIST

With perseverance, Stiefvater taught illustration workshops and became an award-winning colored pencil artist. Clients commissioned her to create animal portraits, and equestrian art was her specialty. While a camera could produce an exact replica of the subject, Stiefvater believed that it took an artist to truly capture the mood and character of the moment. This philosophy caught on with clients and art lovers as her work was internationally exhibited and collected. Stiefvater also painted things around her, like pets and landscapes. One of her original acrylic collections was the Richmond Series. It highlighted ordinary life in Richmond, Virginia, starting with the summer sun and finishing with the winter night. Stiefvater's sense of humor shone through with her whimsical version of classics such as Leonardo da Vinci's *Vitruvian Man*, Grant Wood's *American Gothic*, and Thomas Gainsborough's *The Blue Boy*. She replaced the faces of these important subjects with cats. The series was titled, Cats of the Old Masters, and some of the paintings sold internationally on eBay for hundreds of dollars.

American Gothic (1930), by Iowa native Grant Wood, is one of the world's most iconic oil paintings. It demonstrates the realism style of fifteenth-century northern European artists and Wood's Puritanistic virtues of Midwestern American culture.

FAMILY LIFE

While Stiefvater was working as a full-time artist, she and Edward had their two children, Victoria and Will. She affectionately called them "Thing 1 and Thing 2." Although she was busy changing diapers, cooking dinner, and doing the laundry, Stiefvater didn't turn down any clients who wanted portraits. To stay fresh, she rotated two projects a day. Another way she avoided burnout was to set aside any money-making projects on Sundays. She would jump into anything that would get her mind off of work. She told Cynthia Leitich Smith of CynLeitichSmith.live journal.com:

> I'm a 26-year old with a serious Peter Pan complex, an addiction to sweet tea and cookie dough, and an obsessive love of music. When I'm not hanging out with my tolerant husband and two toddlers, I'm either writing, reading, rocking out on some sort of musical instrument, creating art or generally frolicking. I'm all about the frolicking.

However, when Monday rolled around again, Stiefvater was back to working twelve-hour days, six days a week. And while she was working as a

BEYOND THE CANVAS

Although Stiefvater did not receive formal training as a portrait artist, she taught herself the skills she needed to achieve her goals. Books, classes, and studying artists became her teachers. She would complete monthly artist studies, learning to work with new mediums, and create a piece in the artist's style. In January 2007, Stiefvater scrutinized the methods and paintings of one of her favorite portrait painters, John Singer Sargent (1856–1925). After numerous sketches and a full-color study, she put brush to canvas and painted *Horses of Roan*. Stiefvater noted it was the closest visual of water horses she'd had.

These artist studies offered valuable lessons. Contrast allowed the artist to guide the viewer's attention to see particular details in the artwork. For example, a moonlight scene could have a bright firecracker detailed in the sky. Also, the focal point of artwork should get the most detail. The rest of the content can become less specific as it moves away from the focal point. It's as if the artist is pointing to the focal point saying, "Look here." Finally, finishing the edges of objects gives them a purposeful look.

When she first began writing, she would study established authors' books, looking for the techniques that made their works so captivating.

Sometimes she would read the first page of favorite novels and then start her own beginning. Stiefvater took these techniques beyond the canvas and applied them to her novels. In *Shiver*, Sam and Grace are detailed more than any other characters. They are also opposites in personality, adding contrast. To gain that all-important finish, Stiefvater smoothed out the transitions between scenes and chapters. Using these techniques and an emotional hook enabled her to create intriguing tension with a masterful touch.

professional artist, she never lost sight of her dream of becoming a best-selling author. She was determined to quit her job someday and write full-time. One way that Stiefvater improved her skills was by working with Tessa Gratton as critique partners. Stiefvater introduced Gratton to fellow author Brenna Yovanoff and within a few short months, the trio was inseparable as a writing team.

THE MERRY FATES

In May 2008, the "Merry Fates" launched a collaborative blog called *Merry Sisters of Fate*. The Merry Fates hoped to use this format to sharpen their YA short story–writing skills. Combining humor and

The Merry Sisters of Fate include Tessa Gratton (*left*), Brenna Yovanoff (*middle*), and Stiefvater (*right*). Although the three authors live in various parts of the United States, they often get together for literary and social events.

romance, torment and magic, their tales explored humanity and mythical creatures. Each writer took turns posting stories, many of which were first drafts. Stiefvater was known for setting a one-hour timer in order to complete her submissions before posting them. Stiefvater, Gratton, and Yovanoff quickly learned that the stories with more audience interaction had stronger endings. This was a lesson they would not soon forget as some of the short stories evolved into novels. Stiefvater's *The Scorpio Races* was once a *Merry Sisters of Fate* short story. The Merry Sisters of Fate put together two hybrid anthologies featuring a compilation of posts from their blog: *An Infinite Thread – A Merry Sisters of Fate Anthology* and *The Curiosities: A Collection of Stories*. Overall, the joint venture taught the ladies the difference between what was fulfilling to them as writers and what was fulfilling to their readers. While the Merry Fates moved on to other projects as award-winning authors, they remain critique partners to this day.

When Stiefvater wasn't busy being a wife, mother, artist, and blogger, she submitted several of her short stories to anthologies such as *Kiss Me Deadly*, *Le maître de Rampling Gate et autre nouvelles*, and *Demons: Encounters with the Devil and His Minions, Fallen Angels, and the Possessed*. On top of that, she chiseled out two hours every Wednesday to write her novel. She would make herself some sweet tea and settle in with her laptop, Orlando, or her desktop computer, Darcy, to work on a manuscript she had started years earlier. It had been sent to publishers then—skipping the agent process because she wanted to do it herself. Although Stiefvater had received rejection letters, she was delighted when a revision request from Flux editor Andrew Karre came in the mail. He believed the manuscript needed to be tighter, in an older voice, and edgier. By her own admission, Stiefvater didn't take the revisions as far as she could have at the time. Because of this, Flux did not buy the manuscript. Stiefvater wasn't disappointed, though. She knew she was close to her goal.

Determined to rework the manuscript as an adult, Stiefvater jumped back into her childhood obsession with homicidal fairies and myth and legend. Because the novel had already been labeled as paranormal fiction, the challenge was to stay ahead of the reader. She rewrote the first three chapters, adding angst, romance, and dimension to her characters. She tacked on two more hours each week as she neared completion. It took four months, but she finally finished *The Queen's Bidding*. Just a few months later, Stiefvater had a contract for what is now known as *Lament: The Faerie Queen's Deception*. The book was released in October 2009, and she made enough money with the advance to buy a new mattress. The sequel, *Ballad: A Gathering of Faerie*, was released the following year. *Requiem*, the third in the *Books of Faerie* series is expected in 2014.

After finishing the manuscript for *Lament*,
Stiefvater began working on a standalone called
The Horses of Roan. Set in Virginia's marshland, this
supernatural thriller told the tale of Irish *capaill uisce*,
water horses with a hint of shape-shifting. Although
her skills as a writer were improving, she deemed
the manuscript a disastrous mess. With meaning-
less magic and a plot angle that left much to be
desired, the novel could have been written by any-
one. It lacked her special style, and Stiefvater hadn't
quite reached the level of writing she wanted to. *The
Horses of Roan* was put on hold. The time had come
for Stiefvater to write the series that put her on the
YA best-seller list.

THREE

CHAPTER

WEREWOLVES ARE THE NEW VAMPIRES

The Harry Potter, *Hunger Games*, and *Twilight* series rocked the YA literary world, filling it with a modern-day approach to magic, intrigue, and mystery. Readers couldn't get enough of battling wizards, postapocalyptic survival, and love-struck vampires. When the first book in Stiefvater's *Shiver* trilogy hit bookstores, readers went gaga. They couldn't get enough of its shape-shifting werewolves imprisoned by the cold, snowy winters of Mercy Falls. Stiefvater's fresh approach to magic and myth made werewolves the new vampires.

PLOTTING A STORY

But like many successful novels, it only takes a focal point to get the story

Suzanne Collins's *The Hunger Games* trilogy has sold over fifty million print and digital copies. This international best-seller features a rebel heroine who finds herselin a deadly battle to entertain the postapocalyptic Panem nation.

started. For Stiefvater, she was inspired by Audrey Niffenegger's *The Time Traveler's Wife*. Not prone to crying, Stiefvater couldn't help herself each time she reread the novel. She couldn't shake the effect it had on her, and this was exactly what she wanted for her next novel. Stiefvater wanted her readers to reach for a box of tissues, immersing themselves in the characters, the opposition that surrounded them, and the fine balance between light and heavy emotional moments. She was ready to write, but the story line never came. She had a case of writer's block. Andrew Karre, her Flux editor, suggested entering a short story contest. This would help get the creativity flowing while generating buzz for *Lament*. The only contest available at the time was focused on two-thousand-word werewolf stories. Stiefvater was unimpressed. Werewolves were not her favorite subject, but she decided to give it a whirl. Inspiration evaded her that day, but at night, the plot for "Still Wolf Watching" appeared in her dreams.

Immediately jotting down what she saw in her dream, Stiefvater had her plot. Unlike the werewolves of science fiction and horror, her werewolves had become metaphors for the loss of one's identity. Believing in choice despite circumstances, Stiefvater wanted her main characters, Sam and Grace, to take on challenges and risks with maturity. Toying with character building, teenage angst, and the mysteries of nature, it took Stiefvater five months to write what would eventually become the first book in the the *Shiver* trilogy. When she received a call that *Shiver* had hit the best-seller list, Stiefvater blew away. Her hand wouldn't stop shaking; she finally achieved her dream of becoming a best-selling YA author. Stiefvater told Sue Corbett

Occasionally, Maggie Stiefvater reflects on her literary success and considers what she would tell her beginning-writer self. One of the things she would advise is to laugh at those who say it can't be done.

of PublishersWeekly.com, "Many things I have done have failed to render my parents speechless but when I called my father to tell him I had hit the *New York Times* best-seller list, I finally rendered him speechless. It was a very satisfying moment."

CREATING A SERIES

Shiver was intended to be a stand-alone novel, but Stiefvater found that there were too many loose ends. As she began plotting out the sequel, *Linger*, she realized that the story arc actually called for three novels. Once she received the thumbs-up to complete what is known today as the *Shiver* trilogy, she began writing *Linger*. As the story unfolded before her, the need for specific elements made itself known to her. Grace's backstory needed to be expounded upon. Cole, a new character to the series, loved verse. Stiefvater included references to Voltaire's *Candide* and Rainer Maria Rilke's poetry, among other prose. Many of her readers would go back and read some of these references. Published in 2010, *Linger* debuted at number one on the *New York Times* best-seller list.

Forever, the third and final book in the *Shiver* trilogy, was written to answer readers' questions. However, when Stiefvater was writing the draft, the mood and tone had left her wanting. She tossed the

J. K. Rowling, best known for the Harry Potter series, began plotting the international best-seller during a delayed train trip in England. After five years of plotting the entire series, she finally sat down to write.

entire thing. To Stiefvater, mood is what brings her back to the computer to write each day. With the mood intact, she rewrote *Forever* from scratch. This time, she nailed it and the book was published in 2011. It was received well by the *Shiver* trilogy fans, but many wrote with questions regarding the ending. While she tries to respond to her fans individually, Stiefvater offered an all-encompassing online video. She noted that as a reader, she loves endings that leave her thinking about the book all day. The *Shiver* trilogy characters are left with endless possibilities, knowing they could do anything with their lives. Ideally, it's a message of hope.

The *Shiver* trilogy was the series that made Stiefvater a YA novelist superstar. With more than 1.7 million copies in print and countless foreign editions, Stiefvater absorbed her readers in a mythical world and the emotional connection between her characters. Some say Stiefvater is the "next big thing," another Stephenie Meyer, Suzanne Collins, or J. K. Rowling. Whether that's true or not, Stiefvater is well on her way to making an impact on the kind of books young adults—and a great number of adults—are reading.

Stiefvater followed up the *Shiver* trilogy with the novel she had always wanted to write. Having traveled to the United Kingdom several times, witnessed

CROSSOVER FICTION

Supernatural YA fiction has been all the rage in books and on film. But it's not just teens that are lining up to get the latest copy of their favorite novel or buy movie tickets to midnight showings. Adults are just as eager. However, this phenomenon, often called crossover fiction, is not new. Adults have been reading YA novels for decades. Often the lines that define YA fiction are blurry. Considered by many to be the quintessential crossover title, Stephenie Meyers's *Twilight* crossed the age divide. Adult women as well as teenaged girls couldn't get enough of the vampire romance. J. K. Rowling's Harry Potter took crossover fiction a step further by erasing gender lines. Men and women, young and old, flocked to get their hands on the novels. Stiefvater believes that the secret to Harry Potter's crossover fiction success is its fictional world. Rowling's masterful skill reached a broad readership, causing fans to fall in love with reading all over again. She shares the following with her M-Stiefvater.livejournal.com readers: "...I think it means that the real power of a crossover title isn't a novel's ability to appeal to both teens and adults. I think the real power of a crossover title is a novel's ability to appeal to a wide range of humans."

animals eating other animals, and yet still infatu-
ated with water horses, she picked up *The Horses
of Roan* and got to work. Stiefvater endeavored to
keep her novel—and all other fantasy works—as
similar to the real world as possible. With only a
minor adjustment here and there, she thought her
readers would recognize and relate to real aspects
and experiences. In turn, this would make her novel
more believable.

The story unfolds on Thisby, an island much like
any dotting the Atlantic Ocean, where horses bound
from the waters to slaughter cattle and humans. She
blended Irish, Manx, and Scottish mythology, often
plagiarizing herself by adding favorite lines from *The
Horses of Roan* to her new manuscript. Stiefvater
introduced a multidimensional emotional hook, a racing element, and old magic. As a fan of fictitious and
tantalizing food descriptions in novels, she "took a
page" from Diana Wynne Jones's 42nd-century but-
ter pies in *A Tale of Time City*. Stiefvater created fluffy
November Cakes topped with a caramel-honey glaze
that were served at the opening event of a folk festival. She later created a real November Cakes recipe
that was published on her blog. Stiefvater wrote on
M-Stiefvater.livejournal.com:

> And of course, finally, in chapter 46 of The
> Scorpio Races, I wrote the scene I'd been

imagining since I was my daughter's age: a herd of water horses tearing in from an angry sea. Chapter 46 isn't a very long one, and it wasn't late when I wrote it, but after I finished the last sentence of it, I closed my computer and had to stop writing for the night. It's a weird feeling to finally do something right after doing it wrong for so many years. I knew before that that The Scorpio Races *was the best thing I'd written so far, but that was when I really realized I'd written the book I'd wanted to find on the shelf all those years ago.*

In 2011 *The Horses of Roan* went on to be published as *The Scorpio Races*. The novel gave Stiefvater an understanding of the delicate balance between realism and metaphor. She said that it was her favorite to date, noting that it dealt with issues that were important to her and it had her signature style.

The Raven Boys, published in 2012, was the next Stiefvater story to find its way to the page. It was one of Stiefvater's thirty unfinished manuscripts from her college days, but she had gotten stuck. Now its time had come. It was the first of a four-part supernatural series called the *Raven Cycle*. Inspired by the tales of King Arthur and the series of Susan Cooper and Lloyd Alexander,

Stiefvater longed to write a series centered on Welsh mythology. This novel, which is aimed at an older audience, tells the tale of star-crossed love. Teens often define themselves by popularity, money, and status, causing them to feel like outsiders if they don't live up to social expectations. Stiefvater uses this as an underlying theme in her book and tosses in a supernatural element. She continues the message with the second book in the *Raven Cycle* series, *The Dream Thieves*.

TELLING LIES FOR A LIVING

F iction is imaginative storytelling, leaving some to say that authors of fiction tell lies for a living. If creating another world filled with compelling characters, intriguing storylines, and multidimensional metaphors is lying, then Maggie Stiefvater wouldn't have it any other way. She has proved that weaving fictitious tales transports her readers into a world of possibility.

BIG CHALLENGES

Writing books that have a profound effect on readers can be challenging. It demands time and focus, often sacrificing other interests in order to tell the story that was meant to be told. Very few writers have the luxury of doing this as a full-time career. Most are part-time at best, working a regular job and fitting in their writing when possible. Although Stiefvater had set a goal

of one day becoming a full-time writer, her responsibilities as a wife, mother, and co-contributor to the
household were great. She wrote when she could,
often while Victoria and Will napped as toddlers. As
they grew, she taught them to respect her "quiet
time" by entertaining themselves. With the success
of *Shiver*, Stiefvater could consider working as a
full-time author. Once she could replace her income,
estimate a three-year income including advances
and royalties, and pay for health insurance, she
stopped working as a full-time artist. While she was
thrilled to realize her goal, she was still putting in
twelve-hour days writing, touring, and managing her
ever-growing social media presence.

But with success comes sacrifice. Stiefvater told
iVillage.ca:

> *Working mothers are not bad mothers.*
> *Women who have a sense of self-identity,*
> *either through a career or through a home-*
> *based activity, are women that kids respect.*
> *My father was on an air craft carrier for six*
> *months out of the year when I was a kid. I*
> *adored him and still do, and what's more —*
> *I'm pretty much just like him. So it's not the*
> *amount of time you spend sitting in the pres-*
> *ence of your kids. It's how you use that time.*

MYTH, MAGIC, AND TRUTH

Maggie Stiefvater's obsession with myth and magic is a driving force in her books. She commented on Guardian.co.uk, "I write about magic in my novels because I want to write about the truth. To me, these are the things that are true about the world: there are heroes and there are villains." As she addresses truth in her books, it is YA fiction that allows her to explore truth through relationships and going against social expectations. For example, the *Shiver* trilogy isn't about teenage Sam losing his human side with every passing winter. The three-book series revolves around a phenomenon Stiefvater witnessed while on school visits. The difference between fifteen-year-olds who expressed themselves as individuals and the clone-like eighteen-year-olds was pronounced. She was shocked and disturbed, believing peer pressure, advertising, and lack of parental influence was at the root of the problem. In order to process what she'd seen, Stiefvater wrote *Shiver* to address this and folded in magic to give it broader truth. When people complain that all teens read these days is fantasy, Stiefvater believes you can't have it be much truer.

One of the ways Stiefvater balances her many responsibilities is by making healthy foods at home. Preservatives, food coloring, and raising agents are what she calls her kryptonite. She is allergic to these ingredients and often finds herself eating at Chipotle Mexican Grill when she's on the road. Their preservative-free food helps sustain her. Stiefvater encourages others—especially writers—to listen to their bodies and avoid those things that cause them to lose focus and feel lethargic or irritable. Even the slightest hint of an additive could prevent the amount of creativity needed to create a future best-seller.

TIME TO UNWIND

Much like she did in her days working as an artist, Stiefvater takes time off to relax and recharge. She joins her kids in outdoor activities, doodles, or goes to the movies. Simply tuning her guitar brings her peace, and drawing allows her to process the world. She welcomes the chance to take on new adventures, as they often give her fresh material for future novels. Faith plays a central role in Stiefvater's life, even though she is reluctant to publicize her beliefs as they could be taken out of context. She is quick to note that her spirituality—not religion—does not affect the characters, content, or language of her novels. It is this spirituality that allows her to take a truthful approach to her writing, revealing the beauty and pain, as well as the choices and consequences, of being human.

As an author who values the importance of setting in her books, Stiefvater also values the setting for her family and her work. For years she had wanted to move deep into Virginia's countryside, despite the inconveniences of living far from others. At one point, she had a chance to either buy a home or a Steinway piano. Today, "Hannibal" the

Named for England's "Virgin Queen," Elizabeth I, Virginia is said to be "the birthplace of a nation." It is known for its historical significance, thriving metropolises, picturesque views, and exclusive distinction in the equestrian world.

piano sits in her music room. But soon, another opportunity presented itself. After ten years of renting, the Stiefvater family bought their first house and moved in May 2012. The New House of Stiefvater, as she calls it, sits amid a patchwork of rolling fields in western Virginia, just miles away from where she was born. With mountains, farm animals, and all the roses, daisies, herbs, peppers, and tomatoes she could possibly plant, Stiefvater is at home. The first room to be unpacked was her office. Her blue desk, leather chair, and yoga ball were placed in the middle, overlooking a big picture window. Family and professional collages lined the walls. Open bookshelves flank an adjacent wall, filled with much-loved books and those she has yet to read. From *The Beatles* to *The Secret Language of Birds* and from *German Poetry in Transition* (1945–1990) to *The Golden Age of Myth and Legend*, Stiefvater has an eclectic collection that continually inspires her fictional writing.

Once at work, ready to churn out a new chapter or a blog post, Stiefvater turns on the tunes. This keeps her focused and far less likely to do laundry, eat cookie dough, or decorate objects using her Sharpie pens. Also, it helps her set that all-important mood for her novels. Stiefvater wants her books to read as if they are movies with accompanying playlists. A scene is likened to a song, and a novel is similar to a playlist, which is made up of various song styles. Together, the novel-turned-playlist is a theme. It is that theme that Stiefvater has to establish before she pounds the keys. For example, when she was strategizing the plot for *Shiver*, she discovered the bittersweet lyrics of the Bravery's "The Ocean." It told of lost love and was the exact mood she needed. The rest of the *Shiver* playlist—used to detail particular scenes in the novel—was made up of songs from Snow Patrol, Imogen Heap, Joshua Radin, and other acoustic singer-songwriters. Stiefvater shared this playlist with her fans on her Web site. This is one of the many ways that she engages her readers. She also includes how-to tips on the craft of writing.

Characters are something Stiefvater strives to perfect, not in the sense of eye color and backstory, but in the sense of how they react and what they desire most. She brings them face-to-face with conflict and observes their reaction. For example, *Shiver*'s Sam was losing his humanity, so Stiefvater created him to have very human actions and decisions that an animal couldn't have or do. She tells her readers on M-Stiefvater.livejournal.com:

I knew all this about Sam before I started writing. I guess what I'm trying to emphasize is that, as a writer, our job is the big picture. You

*can always change the color of the clay you
stick on the arms later. It's the skeleton you
need, so you know how many limbs they have
and whether they walk on two feet or all fours
Big! Think big! It's really easy to get enmeshed
in the details while both writing and editing.
Big swathes first, then refine.*

Writing novels offers Stiefvater little surprises about her characters and hidden truths, often while she's dreaming. For instance, she discovered the first two lines of *Shiver* when Grace whispered them to her in a dream. One of *Forever*'s main characters clued her into his need for nonstop motion, noting that if he stopped running, he wouldn't know what to do. In both cases, Stiefvater woke up and immediately took notes.

While piecing together plots of a novel, Stiefvater uses a concept she learned from a friend called "gimme points." Every writer has a certain number when they start a novel. A gimme point is lost when the reader's confidence wavers because of a convenient plot element, a tragic ending, swear words, or unfamiliar sentence structure. Once they are gone, the reader gives up reading, and this is disastrous. With a list of gimme points in her head, Stiefvater weighs the use of these points for each plot element. She asks herself, "Is that hard-to-pronounce name really worth a point?" or "Is that violent scene worth depleting an entire list of gimme points?"

Every author—no matter how new or established he or she is—revises his or her material. It's a simple equation: manuscript, problem, and solution. When a writer receives revision suggestions from an editor, critique partner, or beta reader, it's his or her job to objectively consider the problem and create a solution. Long, drawn-out descriptions and scenes cost too many gimme points. While editing can take

Maggie Stiefvater is an advocate for ongoing education. She encourages wannabe writers to complete what they've started, noting that despite the many rewrites, the end result will be worth the time and effort.

weeks and even months, it's absolutely crucial to the telling of the story. Stiefvater once cut forty thousand words from the first draft of *The Raven Boys*. She explained on MaggieStiefvater.com:

> *Revision is like water, it's good for everything. You're looking to fix pacing, make characters consistent, make dialog natural, delete unnecessary scenes, tighten themes, eliminate extraneous characters, add connecting scenes. You know what I don't care so much about? Fixing typos. Changing word choice line by line. Making sure that I don't have two Mondays in a row. That stuff will not make or break a book and it's the very last thing you do. Revisions, to me, mean gutting the pig. Big picture. Global. Not line by line.*

Ideally, Stiefvater puts the manuscript away for a month. She forgets about it altogether until it's time for a fresh look. In a professionally bound version, she reads the draft for additional revisions as well as final line and copyediting. While this aspect of writing can be tedious, it does make for a more readable story. Not distracted by pointless scenes and misspelled words, a reader can get lost in the magical world an author has created.

HITTING THE ROAD (IN A '73 CAMARO)

CHAPTER FIVE

One of Maggie Stiefvater's favorite aspects of being a best-selling author is receiving the first copy of one of her novels. Whether they are intended for the United States or are one of thirty-eight foreign editions, she caresses the cover, rereads much-loved sections, and posts it on her social media sites. Still amazed that her YA novels could resonate with readers of various cultures, Stiefvater is honored to share her novels and writing adventures with readers all over the world. In 2010, she had a chance to do just that. With extra novel copies and Sharpie-covered giveaway guitars, she hopscotched her way around the United States before heading overseas to

Loki is known for his cunning, unpredictable ways. He often pits giants, monsters, gods, and heroes against one another. Although Loki is a trickster, his mischievous antics bring much-needed change to the rigid structure of the gods.

the United Kingdom, Germany, Lithuania, France, Bulgaria, and Hungary.

BIG CHANGES

Willing to help out at home with the children, Edward quit his job. This freed Stiefvater to move ahead with the business of being a best-selling author. She and her publicist filled a travel schedule with international interviews, speech writing, videoing award acceptances, auctions, foreign rights deals, and book promotions—some of which were attended in Stiefvater's 1973 Camaro. Named after the Norse god of mischief, "Loki" was a gift the author gave to herself when she sold *Shiver* and became a full-time author. Stiefvater had been surrounded with classic cars throughout her childhood, and she hadn't lost her love for an engine's roar, the smell of gasoline, or feeling the wind in her hair at warp speed.

Rather than taking to the skies for book tours, Stiefvater convinced her publicist to let her use Loki for her *Forever* book tour in July 2011. Known for its numerous breakdowns, Stiefvater had it in the shop for several months, getting the reddish-orange car outfitted for the three-week tour. Not wanting to take on the 3,700 miles (5,955 kilometers) of road alone, Tessa Gratton agreed to join her. While she'd

MULTIMEDIA MEETS SOCIAL MEDIA

Gone are the days of authors simply writing books. Today, authors are expected to reach out and engage their readers using social media. These efforts drive interest and book sales, and Stiefvater embraced this connection with her upbeat personality, dark humor, and multimedia talents.

As a teenager, Stiefvater thought that she'd need to choose between her love of writing, art, and music. However, she learned to intertwine them, and noted the lesson in a MyNorth.com interview with Beth Milligan:

> There's this poem called "The Blind Men and the Elephant" about these five blind men who are each touching a different part of an elephant and guessing what it is. One has a tail, and so he thinks the elephant is a rope. Another one is touching a leg, and so he think it's a tree trunk. But really they're all touching the same animal. I feel like when I do my art, and I write, and I paint, it's the same thing— I'm describing the same animal, just from different sides. Almost all of my ideas get treatment from all of the different medias I have available at my disposal.

Not only does Stiefvater combine her writing and original illustrations, but she composes music to complement her novels. For *Linger*, she composed and arranged "One Thousand Paper Cranes" with the help of her younger sister, Kate Hummel. Then she created the animation using paper cutouts, a variety of craft supplies, and what Stiefvater calls "a little black magic." The multimedia efforts were videoed in a stop-motion book trailer featured on her Facebook, YouTube, and Web site pages for her ever-growing international fan base to enjoy each day.

hoped Loki would be in tip-top shape to travel, it wasn't. Stiefvater sold the 1973 Camaro and replaced it with another Loki. This time it was a blue 1973 Camaro. Stiefvater paid tribute to the original, however, by writing it into *The Raven Boys* as "The Pig." She and Gratton packed the new Loki and hit the road. They were off, in a car with customized Virginia license plates that said "Shiver" for select locations in the United States and Canada. Not only did they sign books and meet adoring fans at bookstores, but they also were able to do some sightseeing along the way. One day was spent at Rainbow Ridge Farms Bed and Breakfast in Onalaska, Wisconsin. The two authors were able to relax and meet the animals on the farm. Stiefvater tried her hand at milking a goat and feeding the rest of the gang with animal crackers. Another day was spent jumping from boulder to boulder, striking the Ringing Rocks of Bucks County, Pennsylvania. With a minor

The boulders of Ringing Rocks Park in Pennsylvania create a bell-like sound when struck. Some claim they are supernatural, as little to no flora or fauna inhabit the unusually warm field of boulders.

air-conditioning mishap outside of Nashville, Tennessee, Loki passed the road trip test with flying colors.

Of course, because Stiefvater is an international best-selling author, she has to leave Loki at home to fly to other countries. In August 2011, she visited four Australian cities and attended the Melbourne Writers Festival. She later spoke at schools in the area. That fall, she, along with her mother and sister, boarded a plane headed for the United Kingdom. Stiefvater was on a deadline. She used the seven-hour flight from Long Island, New York, to get as much done on what she called "Magical Novel" before arriving in London. She and Jonas & Plunkett, the UK band who wrote lyrics for "Summer Girl" based on *Shiver*, were honored guests at a Scholastic U.K. event. An interview and day of school visits followed, but the long train ride provided the perfect

When a novel of hers is released, Maggie often goes on an international book promotion tour. Dublin, Ireland, is shown here.

opportunity to work on her novel. Despite catching a cold, Stiefvater visited schools in Newcastle, England. She then attended a librarian conference in Belfast, Northern Ireland. Then it was off to Dublin for a bookstore event before getting back on a plane to London.

The next morning, she gave a dozen back-to-back radio interviews. The coordinator struck up a conversation with Stiefvater, asking her where she was from. As they continued talking, it was soon discovered that his father, a carpenter, went to Richmond to work in an Irish pub ten or fifteen years ago. It turned out that Stiefvater's band had played for the opening of Siné, an Irish pub in Richmond. With a quick phone call to confirm, it was indeed Stiefvater who was in the band so many years ago.

A BIG MILESTONE

By the time Stiefvater returned home to her family, it was time to party. She was turning thirty. Luxuriating in the day, she realphabetized her bookshelves, went to a Russell Brand show, made cinnamon bread, turned in a manuscript, and purchased three Madeleine L'Engle hardcover novels.

On January 23, 2012, The American Library Association (ALA) announced its Youth Media

Like many celebrity authors, Maggie Stiefvater shares the creative happenings in her career along with humorous and random side stories now and again. However, she strives to maintain privacy when it comes to her family.

Awards. Stiefvater was busy with chores and nearly missed the call from the chairman of the Printz Committee. Although the connection was poor, she realized the chairman was giving her spectacular news. *The Scorpio Races* had won the Michael L. Printz honor. Finally, one of her books had been awarded the same honor that so many of her childhood favorites had been awarded. That same day, another phone call informed her that *The Scorpio Races* won an Odyssey Award. This was the ALA award for excellence in audiobooks.

In the fast lane yet again, Stiefvater spent the rest of 2012 zigzagging her way across the United States. She attended book signings and festivals and met up with the other Merry Sisters of Fate, Tessa Gratton and Brenna Yovanoff. The following year wasn't much different. Obsessed with speed and a lover of racing movies such as *Herbie, Days of Thunder,* and *The Black Stallion*, this author was ready to do a little racing of her own. She bought a Ford Fiesta. It was part of her master plan to rally race on a course of dirt and gravel. Using the opportunity to promote her novel, Stiefvater had *The Raven Boys* book cover bonded to the outside.

Like many prolific writers, Stiefvater continues to be busier than ever with all aspects of writing. She has many obligations to her readers and publishers that keep her hopping. From keeping track of travel itineraries to conferences to finalizing deals for foreign book rights, Stiefvater is one busy author. She writes her own speeches, gives international interviews, films acceptance videos for awards, and still manages to Google herself.

Admittedly obsessed with reviews, she is sure to check a few selected reviewers whom she values. When asked if she's ready for the kind of literary stardom of other prolific YA authors, Stiefvater is humble. She tells YAReads.com:

> It's really bizarre, actually, to think that just a few years ago I was reading the "greats" in YA and now I'm on lists with them. It happened so fast that I still sort of just feel as if my hair is on fire. It's pretty amazing to go into a library, say my name, and have the teen librarian instantly begin nodding her head because she not only knows who you are, but she read your book. It's just sort of crazy and wonderful and intimidating. I have readers! I don't want to let these people down!

SIX

PUTTING ON THE BRAKES

Although Maggie Stiefvater spent several years on tour, she needed to put the brakes on to write. *The Dream Thieves*, the third book in the *Raven Cycle* series, and *Requiem*, the third in the *Books of Faerie* series, awaited completion. Also, Scholastic announced Stiefvater's participation in its seven-book series *Spirit Animals*. She had been considering writing a middle-grade book for Victoria and Will, minus the blood, violence, swearing, and romance. The timing had never been right—until now. This multiplatform fantasy adventure series plans to immerse readers in the fantasy world of Erdas. Four multicultural children will go through a ritual, discovering that they have been chosen for a higher purpose. Each book in the series

Maggie Stiefvater loves to interact with and talk to fans. She often participates in readings and special events all over the United States and the world.

offers interactive gameplay on the *Spirit Animals* Web site. Readers will be able to customize their online heroes, choose spirit animals, and save the fictional world of Erdas. Well-known YA authors have been invited to participate in the writing of each book. The first will be published on September 10, 2013. The second, written by Stiefvater, will be published in January 2014. She plans to incorporate her love of Celtic mythology and animals.

LIGHTS, CAMERA, ACTION!

Maggie Stiefvater has always been a big fan of film adaptations. With blockbusters such as Harry Potter, *The Hunger Games*, and *Twilight* hitting the silver screen, the stage was set for her YA novels to be optioned for film rights. On September 14, 2012, the *Los Angeles Times* announced that New Line Cinema acquired the movie rights to *The Raven Boys*. Stiefvater always envisioned *The Scorpio Races* as a movie, so she was thrilled when it was optioned by Katzsmith Productions/Warner Bros. Although Stiefvater has very limited control in the process, she was adamant that the mood of the book be preserved. In addition, Unique Features/Warner Bros optioned Shiver shortly after the novel was released. However, Stiefvater and the producers had a difference of creative opinion. She discontinued the process, and in 2011, the option lapsed. A release date for *The Scorpio Races* and *The Raven Boys* has yet to be set, leaving Stiefvater to wait a bit longer before hearing, "Lights, camera, action!"

Then there's Stiefvater's longtime goal of writing and illustrating a graphic novel. As a youth, she devoured the pages of her King Arthur graphic novel. Its art was gripping, but its images were intended for adult audiences only. She never lost sight of that goal and still intends to create a YA graphic novel using her illustration skills.

THE PROCESS AND
THE AUDIENCE

Connecting with her teen audience is important to Stiefvater. "I believe we only go round this lifetime once, and I believe in getting to the end of that lifetime with no regrets. I think the saddest story ever is the one that starts 'this is what could've happened,'" she wrote on MaggieStiefvater. com. She has much to say in the way of pursuing one's goals. She admits to having a lack of self-confidence in college despite her successes as a student, but they were temporary triumphs. What really gave her lasting satisfaction was making the decision to be confident, voicing big goals, and living without fear.

Stiefvater believes there's a novel in everyone. They just need to know how to get started. In the simplest of explanations, she says it's about the decision and sitting down to do it. Beyond that, she offers writers of all ages her own how-to tidbits, noting that every writer's process is unique. Before typing chapter one, Stiefvater spends days, even weeks, considering the characters, plot arcs, and ending. Her process, while unique to her, focuses on the doing of it. Once she has a clearer picture, she pulls up a blank document and types the title and date. With schedule in hand, Stiefvater plots out the

One of Maggie Stiefvater's greatest influences is the legend of King Arthur. Arthur is portrayed in this painting standing before the famous "round table" with his men.

time she will take to write each week. It could be a half hour, a chunk of hours, or even full days. Then it's time to plan the novel. While some writers need a lot of organization—outlines, synopsis, and scene lists—Stiefvater simply has an idea, determines the ending, and writes a two-page synopsis. She plans the plot and keeps a dim view of her characters and how they will change through the course of the novel. She only needs to know what her characters need and want. Often a character thinks he wants something when he needs something completely different. To diversify characters, she will have them dictate a brief life history. Stiefvater places great importance on setting and uses extensive hands-on research to help her hone the details. Creating the playlist is next as she establishes the theme and mood for the novel. This may take a few days, but then she's in the zone—often with Peanut, her Jack Russell terrier, sleeping beside her desk.

On her way to her ten-thousand-word goal, Stiefvater experiences a slew of reactions. From excitement to depression, she is trying to piece everything together. It's important to know the purpose of each scene and how it relates to the overall story. She muddles through the uncertainty, eating chocolate and drinking sweet tea, until she hits what she calls the "magic switch." She's in a rhythm at this point and the novel is well on its way. Stiefvater

Stiefvater's social media platforms detail day-to-day events in her life and career, including important updates about her Jack Russell terrier, like the one shown here.

focuses her attention on the word count, not pages, as YA manuscripts are typically between seventy-five thousand and one hundred thousand words.

There are those times when a writer is flooded with great ideas. It's tempting to want to abandon one novel in pursuit of another. This also happens to Stiefvater. It took her some time to understand that there aren't always better ideas, just better ways of developing the characters and telling the story.

However, she has a three-option plan to take care of plot bunnies: write a summary paragraph and file it away; write a short story using the idea; or write a one-page synopsis and file it away. One of the most important keys is that plot bunnies are not bound to a deadline. Stiefvater caged a plot bunny since March 2008. She's written a number of chapters and a synopsis based on the idea in between projects. She wrote on M-Stiefvater.livejournal.com, "And I'm glad that I didn't write it back when I first got the idea, because I am such a better writer now. I could've never given it the nuance that it needed back then. Sometimes putting things away for later is the best thing you can do."

Being a best-selling author isn't always glamorous. Every writer faces challenges throughout the process, and Stiefvater is no different. She takes an honest look at a writer's life, acknowledging the pressures and distractions. From finishing a sequel that should live up to the quality of the first to juggling childcare and from waiting for advances to turning down social invitations, there are many details to handle in the life of an author. Stiefvater embraces the worries and doubts because in the end, she loves her career.

Although Maggie Stiefvater wanted to be many things when she grew up, her lifelong dream was to become a best-selling YA author. Now that she's achieved that goal, she continues to work to move her readers with her writing, art, and music. She told her MaggieStiefvater.com readers:

> *I want to shift people's lives in tiny ways through my stories; convince them that they're all heroes too and make them look at nature and magic in a different way. I love to write, I love to get better at it, and I love that it really lets me do everything else on that list too, if I really want to.*

ON MAGGIE STIEFVATER

Date of birth: November 18, 1981

Birthplace: Harrisonburg, Virginia

Current residence: Virginia

First publication: *Lament: The Faerie Queen's Deception* (2009)

Marital status: Married to Edward Stiefvater

Children: Victoria and Will

College attended: Mary Washington College, class of 2003

ON MAGGIE STIEFVATER'S WORK

Books of Faerie

Lament: The Faerie Queen's Deception. Woodbury, MN: Flux, 2008

Synopsis: Sixteen-year-old Deirdre "Dee" Monaghan is on the verge of discovering she can see fairies. Shy and musically gifted, Dee finds herself drawn to the mysterious and dangerous Luke.

Awards: ALA Popular Paperbacks for Young Adults (2010), ALA Best Books for Young Adults (2010), SIBA Book Award nominee, starred review in *Publishers Weekly*, starred review in *Booklist*, Starred review in *KLIATT*

Ballad: A Gathering of Faerie. Woodbury, MN: Flux, 2009

Synopsis: Bagpiper James Morgan and his best friend, Dee, join a private music conservatory where James's talents attract the attention of part muse, part psychic vampire Nuala. Nuala and Dee are hunted by the Fey, as James is left to contend with the Fey Queen in order to save their lives.

Requiem. Woodbury, MN: Flux, 2014

The Wolves of Mercy Falls Series (aka The *Shiver* Trilogy)

Shiver. New York, NY: Scholastic, 2009

Synopsis: A supernatural romance heats up between Grace, a teenage girl living in Mercy Falls, and Sam, a teenage boy and wolf-by-winter. Danger persists as Sam could lose his humanity forever.

Awards: Debuted at number nine on the *New York Times* best-seller list and stayed there for over forty weeks; Indies Choice Book Award Finalist; ALA Best Books for Young Adults; ALA Quick Pick for Reluctant Readers; Amazon Top Ten Books for Teens; *Publishers Weekly* Best Books (2009; VOYA's Perfect Ten (2009), BDB Top Young Reads (2009); Border's Original Voices pick and finalist; Barnes & Noble 2009 Top Twenty Books for Teens; CBC Children's Choice Awards finalist; SIBA Book Award Finalist (2010); Junior Library Guild Selection; Colorado Blue Spruce Young Adult Nominee; Glamour's Best Book to Curl Up With

Linger. New York, NY: Scholastic, 2010

Synopsis: *Linger* continues the bittersweet romance of Sam and Grace. Former rock star and new addition to the wolf pack, Cole has a secret identity. Unable to control his change, he struggles to be released from a painful past, while Isabel deals with the guilt of losing her brother, letting people into her life, and her increasing attraction to Cole.

Awards: Debuted at number one on the *New York Times* best-seller list; *USA Today* best-seller; *Wall Street Journal* best-seller; ABA best-seller; *L.A. Times* best-seller; Junior Library Guild Selection

Forever. New York, NY: Scholastic, 2011

Synopsis: Wolves are being hunted in Mercy Falls, and the love shared between Grace and Sam is once again threatened. Sam faces a predatory world as it collides in one fateful moment.

Awards: *New York Times* best-seller, Amazon's Best Books of the Month (July 2011)

The Scorpio Races. New York, NY: Scholastic, 2011

Synopsis: Orphaned Sean Kendrick and Kate Connolly are desperate to win the annual race that runs along the beaches of the Scorpio Sea. They risk their lives by riding fairy water horses, which lull their riders into a stupor only to be devoured.

Awards: Michael L. Printz Award Honor (2012), The Odyssey Honor Award for best audio production (2012), *Los Angeles Times* Book Times Award Finalist (2012), ALA Notable Books for Children (2012), *New York Times* Notable Children's Book (2011), *Publishers Weekly* Best Children's Book (2011), Chicago Public Library's Best of the Best (2012), Amazon's Best Books for Teens (2011), *School Library Journal's* Best Books of the Year, *Kirkus* Best Teen Books of the Year (2011), *Horn Book* Best Books (2011), Children's Book Committee Best Children's Books of the Year (2012), Finalist, Mythopoeic Fantasy Award for Children s Literature (2012), YALSA Top Ten Best Fiction for Young Adults (2012), YALSA Amazing Audiobooks for Young Adults (2012), NCTE/ CLA Notable Children's Book in the English Language Arts (2012)

The Raven Cycle
The Raven Boys. New York, NY: Scholastic Press, 2012
Synopsis: Blue Sargent, the daughter of a town psychic, tries to avoid handsome, rich, and popular Richard "Dick" Gansey. However, she is caught up in the Raven Boy world at prestigious Aglionby

Academy. Now, the prediction she's been warned about all of her life could come true.

Awards: *New York Times* best-seller, *USA Today* best-seller, ABA best-seller, *Time* magazine Season's Most Anticipated Reads, *Publishers Weekly* Best Books (2012), Junior Library Guild Selection, Amazon Books Editors' Selection: Fall Favorites, YALSA Top Ten Best Fiction for Young Adults (2013), Kids' Indie Next List Pick (2012), AudioFile Earphones Award, Audiofile's Best Audiobooks of the Year (2012), Indigo Top 25 (2012), BCCB Blue Ribbons (2012)

The Dream Thieves. New York, NY: Scholastic Press, 2013

Synopsis: Things have changed for Aglionby Academy students—Ronan, Blue, Gansey, and Adam—and they will never be the same again.

Awards: *Time* magazine Season's Most Anticipated Reads, Publishers Weekly Best Books of 2012, Junior Library Guild Selection, Amazon Books Editors' Selection: Fall Favorites, 2013 YALSA Top Ten Best Fiction for Young Adults, Autumn 2012 Kids' Indie Next List Pick, Winner of AudioFile Earphones Award, Audiofile's Best Audiobooks of the Year for 2012, Indigo Top 25 of 2012, BCCB Blue Ribbons 2012

"Having published six novels in four years and showing no signs of stopping, 'Stiefvater has established herself as one of the finest YA novelists writing today.'" – *Entertainment Weekly*

Lament: The Faerie Queen's Deception
"Vibrant and potent, YA readers searching for faerie stories will be happy to find this accomplished debut novel." – *Publishers Weekly, starred review*, 2008

"This beautiful and out-of-the-ordinary debut novel, with its authentic depiction of Celtic Faerie lore and dangerous forbidden love in a contemporary American setting, will appeal to readers of Nancy Werlin's *Impossible* and Stephenie Meyer's *Twilight* series." – *Booklist, starred review*, 2008

"Part adventure, part fantasy, and wholly riveting love story, *Lament* will delight nearly all audiences with its skillful blend of magic and ordinary life." – *KLIATT, starred review*, 2008

Ballad: A Gathering of Faerie
"Stiefvater weaves suspense, romance, and music together to deliver a thoroughly satisfying story. Give this one a shot." – *Realms of Fantasy*, 2009

"[James] snaps out witty repartee that teen readers will wish they could reproduce." – *VOYA*, 2009

"Readers of Holly Black's *Tithe* (2002) or Charles de Lint's *The Blue Girl* (2004) will enjoy this rich foray into faerie. The book's backdrop, so firmly rooted in Celtic myth, is scary, mysterious, magical, and horrifying. " – *Booklist*, 2009

"Maggie Stiefvater excels at writing wonderfully complex characters." – *Carrie Ryan, New York Times Bestselling Author of The Forest of Hands and Teeth*, 2009

Shiver

". . . beautifully written, even poetic at times, and a perfect indulgence for readers of all ages." – *BookPage*, 2009

"Stiefvater leaves the faeries of *Lament* and *Ballad* for a lyrical tale of alienated werewolves and first love . . . her take on werewolves is interesting and original while her characters are refreshingly willing to use their brains to deal with the challenges they face." – *Publishers Weekly, starred review*, 2009

". . . beautiful and moving . . . The mythology surrounding the wolf pack is clever and so well written that it seems perfectly normal for the creatures to exist in today's world. A must-have that will give Bella and Edward a run for their money." – *School Library Journal, starred review*, 2009

"If you are a fan of *Twilight*, then you will love *Shiver*. Beautifully written, with alternating chapters from Grace and Sam's points of view, this a wonderful debut." –*Observer*, 2009

Linger

"This sequel's poetic prose skillfully captures the four teens' longings for love, forgetting, remembering, righting wrongs and life itself. The riveting ending will leave readers panting for the next sequel." – *Kirkus*, 2010

"If *Shiver* left fans wanting more, *Linger* will have them begging." – *Romantic Times*, 2010

"Like *Shiver*, this is a real page turner. These werewolves are not supernatural and the scientific normalcy of being a wolf provides a fascinating turn of events." – *Children's Literature*, 2010

"This riveting narrative, impossible to put down, is not only an excellent addition to the current fangs and fur craze but is also a beautifully written romance that, along with *Shiver*, will have teens clamoring for the third and final entry." – *VOYA*, 2010

Forever

"Now, finally, things come to an epic, romantic, and action-packed close in *Forever*." – *Ellegirl.com*, 2011

"The love between Grace and Sam grows stronger and stronger, and the pain of their plight is palpable and heart-wrenching." – *School Library Journal*, 2011

"[F]illed with suspense, sorrow, and just enough romance…" – *Seventeen Magazine*, 2011

"[A]n intelligent paranormal romance that surreptiously folds in serious adolescent issues, including teens' relationships with their parents, suicidal ideation, morphing bodies and young love." – *Los Angeles Times*, 2011

The Scorpio Races
"[Stiefvater] not only steps out of the young adult fantasy box with *The Scorpio Races* but crushes it with pounding hooves…If *The Scorpio Races* sounds like nothing you've ever read, that's because it is." –*New York Times Book Review*, 2011

"Masterful. Like nothing else out there now." – *Kirkus, starred review*, 2011

"…a study of courage and loyalty tested . . . an utterly compelling read." – *Publishers Weekly, starred review*, 2011

"A book with cross-appeal to lovers of fantasy, horse stories, romance, and action-adventure, this seems to have a shot at being a YA blockbuster."
– *Booklist, starred review*, 2011

"…gets better and better…all the way, in fact, to best."
– *Horn Book, starred review*, 2011

The Raven Boys
"…one of the "season's most anticipated reads…" –
Time, 20112

"My love for Maggie Stiefvater's *The Raven Boys* is so great…Everything in this book feels so grounded and real, by the time the actual magic comes into the story, it is absolutely believable." – *VH1.com*, 2012

"Simultaneously complex and simple, compulsively readable, marvelously wrought. The only flaw is that this is Book 1; it may be months yet before Book 2 comes out." – *Kirkus*, 2012

"It's a tour de force of characterization, and while there is no lack of event or mystery, it is the way Stiefvater's people live in the reader's imagination that makes this such a memorable read." – *Publishers Weekly*, 2012

1981 Heidi Hummel is born on November 18 in Harrisonburg, Virginia.

2001 She meets her future husband, Edward Stiefvater.

2003 Maggie Stiefvater graduates from Mary Washington College with a bachelor of arts.

2008 The *Merry Sisters of Fate* blog is launched.

Lament: The Faerie Queen's Deception is released.

An Infinite Thread – A Merry Sisters of Fate Anthology, Volume 1 is published.

2009 *Shiver* is released in the United States and the United Kingdom.

Ballad: A Gathering of Faerie is released.

2010 *Linger* is published and debuts at number one on the *New York Times* best-seller list.

"The Hounds of Ulster" is included in the short-story anthology *Kiss Me Deadly.*

Stiefvater presents "How Bad Teens Become Famous People" at a TEDxNASA conference in Virginia.

2011 *Forever*, the third and final book in the *Shiver* Trilogy, is released in the United States and United Kingdom.

Stiefvater and Tessa Gratton hit the road in her Loki for a *Forever* book tour in the United States and Canada.

Stiefvater travels to Perth, Melbourne, Sydney, and Brisbane, Australia, for literary events.

"Non Quis, Sed Quid" is published in the short-story anthology *Demons: Encounters with the Devil and His Minions, Fallen Angels, and the Possessed.*

The Scorpio Races novel and audiobook are released.

The *Hollywood Reporter* announces that Katzsmith/Warner Bros. acquired the movie rights to *The Scorpio Races*.

Stiefvater, along with her mother and her sister, goes on a book tour in the United Kingdom.

2012 *The Scorpio Races* is named a Michael L. Printz Honor Book by the American Library Association.

The Scorpio Races wins an Odyssey Honor.

The Stiefvaters move into their new home.

The Curiosities: A Collection of Stories a compiled anthology featuring stories from Maggie Stiefvater, Tessa Gratton, and Brenna Yovanoff is published.

The *Los Angeles Times* announces that New Line Cinema has acquired movie rights to *The Raven Boys*.

The Raven Boys is released.

2013 Scholastic announces Stiefvater will be writing the second of seven books in its multiplatform series *Spirit Animals*.

Stiefvater drives a race car with a decal of *The Raven Boys* book cover.

The Dream Thieves, the second book in the *Raven Cycle* series, is released.

2014 Stiefvater's *Spirit Animals* novel, the second in the multiplatform series, will be published.

Requiem, the third in the *Books of Faerie* series, is expected to hit bookstores.

ADVANCE Money paid by a publisher for the rights to publish a book.

AGENT A person who represents a writer in securing publication.

ANTHOLOGY A collection of literary works, such as short stories, plays, poems, songs, excerpts from novels, essays, and articles.

BACKSTORY The historical events of a character or situation leading up to the opening of a short story or novel.

BETA READERS A person who corrects the grammar, spelling, style, and characterization of a fictional work prior to publication.

BOOK TRAILER Similar to a movie trailer, a book trailer is a presentation used for book promotion.

COPYEDITING The process of improving the format, style,and accuracy of literature before its publication.

CRITIQUE PARTNER A person with whom a writer exchanges originally written literature in order to receive feedback.

DRAFTS An unfinished or unpolished copy of a written manuscript.

EDITOR A person who assigns and perfects written material in order to be published.

EPIC A poem that describes the adventures of heroic or legendary characters.

FANTASY FICTION Fiction containing elements such as magic and mythological creatures that do not exist in the real world.

FICTION Invented narrative that can be inspired by real people, experiences, or events.

GRAPHIC NOVEL A novel that uses sequential illustrations to tell a fictional story.

HOOK A phrase, sentence, or paragraph used to grab the reader's attention.

MANUSCRIPT From the Latin *manu scriptus,* meaning "written by hand." An unpublished work of fiction or nonfiction.

MULTIPLATFORM SERIES Books, television programs, video games, podcasts, and mobile applications created to support a publisher's series.

MYTHOLOGY A collection of traditional stories expressing the beliefs, values, or history of a group of people.

PACING The speed of a literary work.

PARANORMAL FICTION Also known as speculative fiction, this type fiction includes ghosts, aliens, shape-shifters, vampires, werewolves, and other creatures of fantasy.

PLOT An overview of a short story or novel.

PLOT BUNNIES One or more story ideas that haunt a writer until they are written in a piece of literature.

PUBLICIST A person who creates and manages publicity for a literary or entertainment personality.

ROYALTIES Money contractually paid to the creator of a copyrighted or patented work.

SHORT STORY A short piece of fiction containing a limited number of characters and words.

STANDALONE A book that is not part of a series.

THRILLER A book or film known for its suspense, action, quick pace, and multidimensional plots.

WRITER'S BLOCK An author's inability to write because of a lack of creativity or inspiration.

YA FICTION Also known as young adult fiction, this genre is written for a twelve- to eighteen-year-old audience.

American Library Association (ALA)
50 E. Huron Street
Chicago, IL 60611
(800) 545-2433
Web site: http://www.ala.org
Since 1876, the American Library Association has
    been the oldest and largest library association
    in the world. The Young Adult Library Services
    Association (YALSA), a division of ALA, offers
    quality library services to teens. It also awards
    excellence in literature with Newbery (children's
    books), Caldecott (illustrated children's books),
    and Printz (YA books) honors.

Flux
2143 Wooddale Drive
Woodbury, MN 55125-2989
(877) 639-9753
Web site: http://www.fluxnow.com
Flux publishes YA fiction that offers an honest explo-
    ration of life using comedy and tragedy, as well as
    joy and pain.

New York Times Company
620 Eighth Avenue
New York, NY 10018
(212) 556-1234
Web site: http://www.nytimes.com/best-sellers-
    books/overview.html
The New York Times Company is a leading multi-
    media news company reaching an international

audience. Every week, the *New York Times* lists the best-sellers of fiction and nonfiction literature.

Running Press Kids
2300 Chestnut Street, Suite 200
Philadelphia, PA 19103
(215) 567-5080
Web site: http://www.perseusbooksgroup.com
    /runningpress
A member of Perseus Books Group, Running
    Press distributes books and book-related kits.
    International divisions of Perseus Books include
    Publishers Group Canada and Perseus Running
    Press in the United Kingdom and Europe.

Scholastic Inc.
557 Broadway
New York, NY 10012
(800) 724-6527
Web site: http://www.scholastic.com
Scholastic is the largest publisher and distributor of
    children's books, technology, media, and maga-
    zines in the world. It serves customers in over
    150 countries, including Scholastic Canada and
    Scholastic UK.

TED Conferences, LLC
250 Hudson Street, Suite 1002
New York, NY 10013
(212) 346-9333
Web site: http://www.ted.com

Since 1984, TED has been sharing "ideas worth
    spreading" with the help of awe-inspiring intel-
    lectuals working in technology, entertainment, and
    design. TEDx, one of TED's divisions, offers pre-
    sentations in small group settings.

University of Mary Washington
1301 College Avenue
Fredericksburg, VA 22401
(540) 654-1000
Web site: http://www.umw.edu
A women's college founded in 1908, this public liberal
    arts and sciences institution has evolved to meet
    the needs of international students. Once known
    as Mary Washington College, the University of
    Mary Washington is a coed university offering
    undergraduate and graduate programs.

WEB SITES

Due to the changing nature of Internet links, Rosen
Publishing has developed an online list of Web sites
related to the subject of this book. This site is updated
regularly. Please use this link to access the list:

http://www.rosenlinks.com/AAA/stief

Alexander, Lloyd. *The Chronicles of Prydain*. New York, NY: Square Fish, 2011.

Briggs, Katharine. *An Encyclopedia of Fairies: Hobgoblins, Brownies, Bogies, and Other Supernatural Creatures*. New York, NY: Pantheon Books, 1978.

Bullfinch, T. *The Golden Age of Myth and Legend*. Hertfordshire, England: Wordsworth Editions, 1998.

Cooper, Susan. *The Dark Is Rising Sequence: Over Sea, Under Stone; The Dark Is Rising; Greenwitch; The Grey King; Silver on the Tree*. New York, NY: Margaret K. McElderry Books, 2013.

Dashner, James. *Infinity Ring Book 1: A Mutiny in Time*. New York, NY: Scholastic, 2012.

De La Pena, Matt. *Infinity Ring Book 4: Curse of the Ancients*. New York, NY: Scholastic, 2013.

Farley, Walter. *The Black Stallion*. New York, NY: Random House Books for Young Readers, 1986.

Godin, Seth. *The Dip: A Little Book That Teaches You When to Quit (and When to Stick)*. New York, NY: Penguin Group, 2007.

Henry, Marguerite. *Marguerite Henry Treasury of Horses: Misty of Chincoteague, Justin Morgan Had a Horse, King of the Wind*. New York, NY: Aladdin, 2007.

Jones, Diana Wynne. *Charmed Life*. New York, NY: HarperCollins, 2009.

Jones, Diana Wynne. *Dogsbody*. New York: NY: Firebird, 2012.

Jones, Diana Wynne. *Fire and Hemlock*. New York, NY: Firebird, 2012.

Jones, Diana Wynne. *The Lives of Christopher Chant*. New York, NY: Harper Trophy, 2007.

Jones, Diana Wynne. *A Tale of Time City*. New York, NY: Firebird, 2012.

Kirby, Matthew J. *Infinity Ring: Book 5*. New York, NY: Scholastic Inc., 2013.

L'Engle, Madeleine. *A Wrinkle in Time*. New York, NY: Farrar, Straus and Giroux, 2010.

Lewis, C. S. *Chronicles of Narnia Box Set*. New York, NY: HarperCollins, 2010.

McMann, Lisa. *Infinity Ring Book 3: The Trap Door*. New York, NY: Scholastic, Inc., 2013.

Melin, Charlotte. *German Poetry in Transition (1945–1990)*. Lebanon, NH: University Press of New England, 1999.

Nielsen, Jennifer A. *Infinity Ring: Book 6*. New York, NY: Scholastic, Inc., 2013.

Niffenegger, Audrey. *The Time Traveler's Wife*. Orlando, FL: Houghton Mifflin Harcourt, 2004.

Nozedar, Adele. *The Secret Language of Birds*. New York, NY: Harper Element, 2006.

Riordan, Rick. *The 39 Clues Complete Collection Book 1–11*. New York, NY: Scholastic, Inc. 2012.

Ryan, Carrie. *Infinity Ring Book 2: Divide and Conquer*. New York, NY: Scholastic, Inc. 2012.

Shakespeare, William. *A Midsummer Night's Dream*. Philadelphia, PA: Empire Books, 2012.

Voltaire. *Candide*. New York, NY: CreateSpace Independent Publishing Platform, 2013.

Alison. "Author Interview and Book Giveaway: Linger by Maggie Stiefvater." Alison's Book Marks, 2010. Retrieved February 5, 2013 (http://www .alisonsbookmarks.com/2010/07/author-interview -and-book-giveaway.html).

Angiegirl. "Shiver Blog Tour: Interview with Maggie Stiefvater + Giveaway!" Angieville, 2009. Retrieved February 2, 2013 (http://www.angie-ville.com/2009/ 08/shiver-blog-tour-interview-with-maggie.html).

bclement412. "Linger Blog Tour Part 2 and 3: Review// Interview//WINNER." Abyss, 2010. Retrieved February 23, 2013 (http://bclement412.blogspot .mx/2010/07/linger-blog-tour-part-2-and-3.html).

Book Beast. "Maggie Stiefvater Talks New Novel 'The Raven Boys,' Fast Cars, and YA Fiction." 2012. Retrieved February 22, 2013 (http://www. thedailybeast.com/articles/2012/09/28/maggie-stief- vater-talks-new-novel-the-raven-boys -fast-cars-and-ya-fiction.html).

Booklist Online. "Maggie Stiefvater Interview." 2009. Retrieved February 23, 2013 (http://youtu.be/ IRhu076hM64).

Corbett, Sue. "Q & A with Maggie Stiefvater." *Publishers Weekly*, 2011. Retrieved January 27, 2012 (http://www.publishersweekly.com/pw/ by-topic/authors/interviews/article/48971-q -a-with-maggie-stiefvater.html).

thedarkphantom. "Interview with Maggie Stiefvater, author of LINGER." The Dark Phantom Review, 2010. Retrieved February 23, 2013 (http://

thedarkphantom.wordpress.com/2010/07/22/
interview-with-maggie-stiefvater-author-of-linger).

DeSmyter, D. J. "Author Interview: Maggie Stiefvater/
Giveaway by D. J. D." DJ DeSmyter, 2010. Retrieved
February 22, 2013 (http://www.djwrites.com/2010/
07/author-interview-maggie.html).

Drahos, Marta Hepler. "Fantasy Writer Makes Real
Impact on Fiction Genre." National Writers
Series, 2012. Retrieved March 3, 2013 (http://
nationalwritersseries.org/fantasy-writer-makes
-real-impact-on-fiction-genre/).

Galleys Smith. "Interview: Maggie Stiefvater." 2010.
Retrieved February 22, 2013 (http://www.galley-
smith.com/2010/07/16/interview-maggie
-stiefvater).

iVillage. "Work After Baby: Inspiring Moms – From
Actors to Athletes – Share Their Tales." Retrieved
March 6, 2013 (http://www.ivillage.ca/parenting/
celebrity-mamas/work-after-baby-inspiring-moms
-actors-to-athletes-share-their-tales).

Johnson, Joanne. "Interview with YA author, Maggie
Stiefvater." Write, Right?, 2010. Retrieved January
27, 2013 (http://joanneprushing.wordpress.com).

Kate. "Interview with Maggie Stiefvater and Giveaway!"
Read This Book!, 2010. Retrieved February 22, 2013
(http://readthisbook.wordpress.com/2010/07/23/
interview-with-maggie-stiefvater).

Kit, Borys. "New Line Picks Up Maggie Stiefvater's
YA Novel 'The Raven Boys.'" *Hollywood
Reporter,* 2012. Retrieved January 22, 2013

(http://www.hollywoodreporter.com/heat-vision/
new-line-raven-boys-maggie-stiefvater-370454).

Lavender Lines. "Q & A with Maggie Stiefvater AND a
Linger Giveaway!!!!" 2010. Retrieved February 22,
2013 (http://lavenderlines.wordpress.com/2010/
07/23/q-a-with-maggie-stiefvater-and-a-linger-
giveaway).

"A Life Bound by Books." "Blog Tour: Interview with
Author Maggie Stiefvater + a Contest!! 2010.
Retrieved February 22, 2013 (http://
alifeboundbybooks.blogspot.mx/2010/07/blog
-tour-interivew-with-author-maggie.htm

Lodge, Sally. "PW Talks with Maggie Stiefvater."
Publishers Weekly, 2012. Retrieved January 23,
2013 (http://www.publishersweekly.com/pw/
by-topic/authors/interviews/article/52295-pw
-talks-with-maggie-stiefvater.html).

loreleimarsh. "Author Interview & Giveaway with Maggie
Stiefvater." Tattooed Books, 2010. Retrieved
January 30, 2012 (http://lisettebes.blogspot.
mx/2010/07/author-interview-giveaway-with
-maggie.html).

Lori. "Q & A and Giveaway with Maggie Stiefvater!!"
Pure Imagination, 2010. Retrieved February
22, 2013 (http://www.pureimaginationblog.
com/2010/07/o-and-giveaway-with-maggie
-stiefvater.html).

"Maggie Stiefvater—Really, It's Me." Facebook,
2013. Retrieved March 5, 2010 (https://www
.facebook.com/MaggieStiefvaterAuthorPage/
app_303682043041415).

Mallis, Frankie Diane. "Maggie Stiefvater Interview." First Novels Club, 2009. Retrieved February 5, 2013 (http://www.firstnovelsclub.com/2009/08/maggie-stiefvater-interview.html).

Margaret Thatcher Foundation. "Chronology." Retrieved December 28, 2012 (http://www.margaretthatcher.org/chronology/default.asp).

Margolis, Rick. "The Mane Event: Maggie Stiefvater on Success, Rejection, and Her New Novel, 'The Scorpio Races.'" *School Library Journal,* 2012. Retrieved February 23, 2013 (http://www.school libraryjournal.com/slj/articles/interviews/893044 -338/the_mane_event_maggie_stiefvater.html.csp).

Milligan, Beth. "Northern Michigan and the Traverse City National Writers Series Welcomes Critically Acclaimed Author Maggie Stiefvater." MyNorth, 2012. Retrieved December 27, 2012 (http:// www.mynorth.com/My-North/September-2012/ Traverse-City-National-Writers-Series-Featuring -Maggie-Stiefvater).

Morgan. "Introducing…Spirit Animals!" On Our Minds, 2013. Retrieved January 22, 2013 (http:// oomscholasticblog.com/2013/01/introducing -spirit-animals.html).

Mountie9. "Interview with Maggie Stiefvater and Contest." Misbehaving Librarian, 2010. Retrieved February 15, 2013 (http://www.misbehavinlibrarian .com/2010/07/interview-with-maggie-stiefvater -and.html).

NPR. "Doomed Love And Psychic Powers In 'Raven Boys.'" 2012. Retrieved January 22, 2013

(http://www.npr.org/2012/09/16/161107554/
doomed-love-and-psychic-powers-in-raven-boys).

Nikki. "Author Interview: Maggie Stiefvater." YA
Reads, 2010. Retrieved February 5, 2013 (http://
www.yareads.com/author-interview-maggie
-stiefvater-2/author-interviews/2750).

Nikki. "Lament: The Faerie Queen's Deception." YA
Reads, 2009. Retrieved February 5, 2013 (http://
www.yareads.com/q-a-with-maggie-stiefvater/
author-interviews/821).

Prather, Eisha, and Jules Danielson. "7-Imp's 7
Kicks #77: Featuring Maggie Stiefvater." Seven
Impossible Things Before Breakfast, 2008.
Retrieved March 1, 2013 (http://blaine.org/
sevenimpossiblethings/?p=1421).

Rosenfeld, Laura. "Exclusive Interview: Maggie
Stiefvater." *Seventeen*, 2012. Retrieved February
3, 2013 (http://www.seventeen.com/entertainment/
features/maggie-stiefvater-interview).

Saya. "Words with Maggie: On Faith, Time-Travel,
and Spoons." The Rock Pool, 2010. Retrieved
February 22, 2013 (http://therockpool.wordpress.
com/2010/07/25/words-with-maggie-on-faith
-time-travel-and-spoons).

Scholastic Canada: Authors & Illustrators.
"Conversation with Maggie Stiefvater." Retrieved
February 2, 2013 (http://www.scholastic.ca/
authors/stiefvater_m).

Showbiz Shelly. "My Interview with Author Maggie
Stiefvater." B96.com, 2012. Retrieved February
23, 2013 (http://b96.cbslocal.com/2012/09/21/
my-interview-with-author-maggie-stiefvater).

Smith, Cynthia Leitich. "Author Interview: Maggie Stiefvater on *Lament: The Faerie Queen's Deception.*" Cynsations, 2008. Retrieved March 1, 2013 (http://cynthialeitichsmith.blogspot.mx/2008/10/author-interview-maggie-stiefvater-on.html).

Stiefvater, Maggie. "2012 Critique Partner Love Connection." Maggie Stiefvater blog, 2012. Retrieved February 8, 2013 (http://maggiestiefvater.com/blog/2012-critique-partner-love-connection).

Stiefvater, Maggie. "An Illustrated Guide to UK Touring, Days 1-3." Maggie Stiefvater blog, 2011. Retrieved February 4, 2012 (http://maggiestiefvater.com/blog/an-illustrated-guide-to-uk-touring-days-1-3).

Stiefvater, Maggie. "Books That Feed Me." Maggie Stiefvater blog, 2010. Retrieved January 27, 2013 (http://maggiestiefvater.com/blog/book-that-feed-me).

Stiefvater, Maggie. "Bring on the Angst, or Confidence: The B Side." Maggie Stiefvater blog, 2009. Retrieved January 30, 2013 (http://maggiestiefvater.com/blog/bring-on-the-angst-or-confidence-the-b-side).

Stiefvater, Maggie. "Death to All Line-Editing: Maggie's Epic Critiquing/Editing Post." Maggie Stiefvater blog, 2009. Retrieved February 8, 2013 (http://maggiestiefvater.com/blog/death-to-all-line-editing-maggies-epic-critiquing-editing-post).

Stiefvater, Maggie. "Dissecting Pages for Mood." Maggie Stiefvater blog, 2011. Retrieved February 20, 2013 (http://maggiestiefvater.com/blog/dissecting-pages-for-mood).

Stiefvater, Maggie. "The Early (Horrible) Writings of
Maggie Stiefvater." Maggie Stiefvater blog, 2009.
Retrieved January 16, 2013 (http://maggiestiefvater
.com/blog/the-early-horrible-writings-of-maggie
-stiefvater).

Stiefvater, Maggie. "From Rough to Final: TEN
Dissections." Maggie Stiefvater blog, 2012.
Retrieved January 21, 2013 (http://maggiestiefvater.
com/blog/from-rough-to-final-ten-dissections).

Stiefvater, Maggie. "Getting an Art Education Online,
Part I." Maggie Stiefvater blog, 2008. Retrieved
March 6, 2013 (http://greywarenart.blogspot.mx/
search?updated-max=2008-05
-01T18:51:00-07:00).

Stiefvater, Maggie. "The Giant Butt-Kicking How to
Write a Novel Post." Maggie Stiefvater blog, 2009.
Retrieved January 29, 2013 (http://maggiestiefvater.
com/blog/the-giant-butt-kicking-how-to-write
-a-novel-post).

Stiefvater, Maggie. "Happy Mother's Day." Maggie
Stiefvater blog, 2008. Retrieved January 27, 2013
(http://greywarenart.blogspot.mx/2008_05_01
_archive.html).

Stiefvater, Maggie. "How to Turn a Novel into a
Textbook." Maggie Stiefvater blog, 2011. Retrieved
March 2, 2013 (http://maggiestiefvater.com/blog/
how-to-turn-a-novel-into-a-textbook).

Stiefvater, Maggie. "In Which I Advocate Caging
Your Plot Bunnies." Maggie Stiefvater blog,
2010. Retrieved February 15, 2013 (http://
maggiestiefvater.com/blog/in-which-i
-advocate-caging-your-plot-bunnies).

Stiefvater, Maggie. "In Which I Talk About Blood, Guts, the F-Bomb, & Your Mom." Maggie Stiefvater blog, 2011. Retrieved March 2, 2013 (http://maggiestiefvater.com/blog/in-which-i-talk-about-blood-guts-the-f-bomb-your-mom).

Stiefvater, Maggie. "In Which Maggie Debates the Meaning of Crossover Fiction." Maggie Stiefvater blog, 2012. Retrieved March 6, 2013 (http://m-stiefvater.livejournal.com/235396.html).

Stiefvater, Maggie. "Knock Knock. Who's There? Peanut." Maggie Stiefvater blog, 2012. Retrieved February 8, 2013 (http://maggiestiefvater.com/blog/knock-knock-whos-there-peanut).

Stiefvater, Maggie. "Linger Song and Purposeful Characterization." Maggie Stiefvater blog, 2010. Retrieved March 2, 2013 (http://maggiestiefvater.com/blog/linger-song-purposeful-characterization).

Stiefvater, Maggie. "Maggie Gets Younger." Maggie Stiefvater blog, 2013. Retrieved March 5, 2013 (http://maggiestiefvater.com/blog/maggie-gets-younger).

Stiefvater, Maggie. "Maggie Stiefvater on Music, Fantasy, and Writing for Herself." Daily Fig, 2011. Retrieved January 2013 (http://dailyfig.figment.com/2011/12/01/maggie-stiefvater-on-music-fantasy-and-writing-for-herself).

Stiefvater, Maggie. "Monday Morning Cup of Tea." Maggie Stiefvater blog, 2008. Retrieved January 27, 2013 (http://greywarenart.blogspot.mx/2008_05_01_archive.html).

Stiefvater, Maggie. "More Wind, Less Snow: Revising for Mood." Maggie Stiefvater blog, 2010. Retrieved

March 2, 2013 (http://maggiestiefvater.com/blog/more-wind-less-snow-revising-for-mood).

Stiefvater, Maggie. "Music and the Working Girl." Maggie Stiefvater blog, 2010. Retrieved March 1, 2013 (http://maggiestiefvater.com/blog/music-and-the-working-girl).

Stiefvater, Maggie. "My Second Post About Food. This Time, Imaginary." Maggie Stiefvater blog, 2011. Retrieved March 2, 2013 (http://maggiestiefvater.com/blog/my-second-post-about-food-this-time-imaginary).

Stiefvater, Maggie. "Novels, on Starting Them." Maggie Stiefvater blog, 2011. Retrieved March 2, 2013 (http://maggiestiefvater.com/blog/novels-on-starting-them).

Stiefvater, Maggie. "On Characters, Knowing Them." Maggie Stiefvater blog, 2011. Retrieved January 30, 2013 (http://maggiestiefvater.com/blog/on-characters-knowing-them).

Stiefvater, Maggie. "The One Where Maggie Buys a Race Car." Maggie Stiefvater blog, 2012. Retrieved January 21, 2013 (http://Maggiestiefvater.Com/Blog/The-One-Where-Maggie-Buys-A-Race-Car).

Stiefvater, Maggie. "The Opposite of Cynical." Maggie Stiefvater blog, 2011. Retrieved January 16, 2013 (http://maggiestiefvater.com/blog/the-opposite-of-cynical).

Stiefvater, Maggie. "The Power of Myth and Magic in Teenage Fiction." Guardian, 2011. Retrieved December 28, 2012 (http://www.guardian.co.uk/books/2011/oct/23/teenage-fiction-myths-and-magic).

Stiefvater, Maggie. "Rather Belayed Butt-Kicking on
    Being a Writer." Maggie Stiefvater blog, 2010.
    Retrieved February 4, 2013 (http://maggiestiefvater
    .com/blog/rather-belayed-butt-kicking-on-being
    -a-writer).

Stiefvater, Maggie. "Reader Questions." Maggie
    Stiefvater blog, 2008. Retrieved March 6, 2013
    (http://greywarenart.blogspot.mx/search?updated
    -max=2008-05-01T18:51:00-07:00).

Stiefvater, Maggie. "Reader Questions About Writing,
    etc." Maggie Stiefvater blog, 2008. Retrieved
    February 22, 2013 (http://greywarenart.blogspot.mx/
    search?q=marriage).

Stiefvater, Maggie. "Remembering." Maggie
    Stiefvater blog, 2008. Retrieved January
    27, 2013 (http://greywarenart.blogspot.mx/
    search?q=dating).

Stiefvater, Maggie. "Remembering Diana Wynne
    Jones." Maggie Stiefvater blog, 2012. Retrieved
    March 1, 2013 (http://maggiestiefvater.com/
    blog/remembering-diana-wynne-jones).

Stiefvater, Maggie. "REVISION: Bring on
    the Clowns, or Revision, Part 1." Maggie
    Stiefvater blog, 2010. Retrieved January
    2013 (http://maggiestiefvater.com/blog/
    revision-bring-on-the-clowns-or-revision-part-1).

Stiefvater, Maggie. "REVISION: The Neverending
    Hamster Wheel of Revising Doom (Reader
    Questions)." Maggie Stiefvater blog, 2010. Retrieved
    March 1, 2013 (http://maggiestiefvater.com/blog/
    revision-the-neverending-hamster-wheel-of-revising
    -doom-reader-questions).

Stiefvater, Maggie. "REVISION: Nothing Is Sacred (Except for the Stuff That Is)." Maggie Stiefvater blog, 2010. Retrieved January 27, 2013 (http://maggiestiefvater.com/blog/revision-nothing-is-sacred-except-for-the-stuff-that-is).

Stiefvater, Maggie. "REVISION: Trouble-Shooting Your Novel." Maggie Stiefvater blog, 2010. Retrieved January 27, 2013 (http://maggiestiefvater.com/blog/revision-trouble-shooting-your-novel).

Stiefvater, Maggie. "Seven Steps to Starting a Novel." Maggie Stiefvater blog, 2010. Retrieved March 2, 2013 (http://maggiestiefvater.com/blog/seven-steps-to-starting-a-novel).

Stiefvater, Maggie. "Shiver, Linger, Forever, Spoiler." Maggie Stiefvater blog, 2012. Retrieved March 1, 2013 (http://maggiestiefvater.com/blog/shiver-linger-forever-spoiler).

Stiefvater, Maggie. "Solving for X. Maggie Stiefvater blog, 2012. Retrieved February 8, 2013 (http://maggiestiefvater.com/blog/solving-for-x).

Stiefvater, Maggie. "Werewolf Nookie & Homicidal Faeries in Several Languages." Maggie Stiefvater blog, 2011. Retrieved March 2, 2013 (http://maggiestiefvater.com/blog/werewolf-nookie-homicidal-faeries-in-several-languages).

Stiefvater, Maggie. "Why I'm a Writer & Not a Fighter Pilot." Maggie Stiefvater blog, 2012. Retrieved February 15, 2013 (http://maggiestiefvater.com/blog/why-im-a-writer-not-a-fighter-pilot/).

Stiefvater, Maggie. "Working Moms and Next, Next, Next." Maggie Stiefvater blog, 2012. Retrieved

January 23, 2013 (http://maggiestiefvater.com/
blog/working-moms-and-next-next-next).

Stiefvater, Maggie. "Writing the Book I Always Meant
To." *M. Stiefvater's Journal*, 2011. Retrieved
March 2, 2013 (http://m-stiefvater.livejournal
.com/217723.html).

Suhr, Paulette. "Interview: Maggie Stiefvater: *Linger-
ing Possibilities*." The Trades, 2010. Retrieved
January 27, 2013 (http://www.the-trades.com/
article.php?id=12023).

Sutton, Roger. "Maggie Stiefvater, Tessa Gratton, &
Brenna Yovanoff Talk with Roger Sutton." *Horn
Book*, 2012. Retrieved January 22, 2013 (http://
www.hbook.com/2012/11/talks-with-roger
/maggie-stiefvater-tessa-gratton-brenna-yovanoff
-talk-with-roger-sutton).

"TEDxNASA - Maggie Stiefvater - How Bad Teens
Become Famous People." You Tube, 2010.
Retrieved February 23, 2013 (http://youtu.be/
glJPg3wfJ1c). Uploaded by TEDxTalks on
Nov 22, 2010).

ABOUT THE AUTHOR

Erin Staley's work ranges from nonfiction books (Rosen Publishing) to copywriting and co-creating and co-facilitating writer workshops with her critique partner. Staley enjoys painting, going to the theater, and frolicking with her pug on Mexico's sandy beaches.

PHOTO CREDITS

Cover, p. 3 Robert Severi/Kate Hummel; pp. 7, 63 Jeff Malet Photography/Newscom; p. 11 Hulton Archive/Getty Images; pp. 14–15, 49, 53, 72 iStockphoto/Thinkstock; p. 17 SFX Magazine/Future/Getty Images; p. 21 Andre Jenny Stock Connection Worldwide/Newscom; p. 26 DEA/M. Carrieri/De Agostini/Getty Images; p. 30 Lisa M. Mandina; p. 35 Studiocanal Filmverleih/dapd/AP Images; p. 37 Bernard Weil/Toronto Star/Getty Images; p. 39 Mike Marsland/WireImage/Getty Images; p. 56 Fine Art Images /SuperStock; p. 60 Allentown Morning Call/McClatchy-Tribune/Getty Images; p. 61 Stockbyte/Thinkstock; p. 67 Anthony Pidgeon/Getty Images; p. 70 Ivy Close Images /Landov; cover and interior pages background (marbleized texture) javarman/Shutterstock.com; cover and interior pages (book) © iStockphoto.com/Andrzej Tokarski; interior pages background (trees) © iStockphoto.com/Artem Efimov.

Designer: Nicole Russo; Editor: Bethany Bryan; Photo Researcher: Amy Feinberg